MW01236192

Raffles flowers

EXECUTIVE EDITOR
Melisa Teo

EDITORS
Joanna Greenfield
Michelle Low

SENIOR DESIGNER
Nelani Jinadasa

ASSISTANT PHOTOGRAPHER
Jonathan Ang

PRODUCTION MANAGER
Sin Kam Cheong

FIRST PUBLISHED IN 2008 BY
Editions Didier Millet Pte Ltd
121 Telok Ayer Street, #03-01
Singapore 068590
edm@edmbooks.com.sg
www.edmbooks.com

Printed in Singapore.

ISBN: 978-981-4217-19-4

COVER
Elegant stands of Siam tulips adorned by single dark pink moth orchid blooms are a visual echo of the stately columns.

PAGE 4
Potted roses evoke the charm of a quintessentially English garden party—in Singapore.

TEXT BY

Ong May Anne

PHOTOGRAPHY BY

Collin Patrick

Editions Didier Millet

introduction

Tropical and temperate; colonial and contemporary. Simple and sumptuous; tall and small. At any given point in time, the flowers of Raffles Hotel are all these and more.

Raffles is a name that has stood for gracious hospitality and colonial charm for over a century. The Hotel is often described as a tranquil oasis in the midst of the modern metropolis that is Singapore. And what would an oasis be without flowers, greenery and the obligatory palm tree? From the lush gardens to the grand hotel lobby and private suites, plants and floral displays abound, quietly breathing life into the stately surroundings.

Much thought is given to how flowers and foliage can best complement the Hotel's distinctive architecture and interiors. With floral arrangements, the obvious solution would be to adhere to a strictly traditional style—that is, arrangements which are full and round in shape, contained in a conventional vase of cut crystal or blue and white china. However, deploying traditional arrangements everywhere and all the time runs the risk of being staid and predictable.

THIS PAGE
A horizontal arrangement of calla lilies and gloriosa lilies interwoven with a base of carnations is ideal for elongated tables.

OPPOSITE
A traditional arrangement is given height by tall stalks of delphiniums, while wispy strands of bear grass add movement.

PAGE 6
Delicate pink hydrangeas and peonies are among the temperate flowers featured at Raffles Hotel.

PAGE 8
Surrounded by wicker, pretty posies with Sweet Akito roses hint at the Hotel's colonial tradition.

THIS PAGE (RIGHT)
Mokara Red orchids on baby's breath in a red glass receptacle show that a simple arrangement can have great visual impact.

THIS PAGE (BELOW)
Twin arrangements of pincushion proteas, moth orchids and ant plants, connected by a horizontal frame of meadow rue twigs.

OPPOSITE
Posies of Leonidas roses, Salmon Bay Peruvian lilies and hypericums are tied with bulrush leaves and secured with pearl pins.

The Resident Florist at Raffles Hotel employs a few clever techniques to circumvent this. He may infuse some modernity into a traditional, round display, for example, by inserting long, clean lines in the form of sweeping stalks of blooms, or a tall, straight vase. Besides vases, other containers may also be used, including coloured glass bowls and shooter glasses. Then there are subtle but clearly contemporary notes, such as the use of stems, leaves and grasses to bind an arrangement, and decorative yet functional items such as berries and pearl pins.

Another way to inject variety is through the choice of flowers. Traditionally, only temperate flowers were used, in keeping with English style, and to this day, many of the Raffles flowers are imported from Holland and New Zealand. However, the Singaporean climate can be unkind to flowers like roses, peonies and hydrangeas. For this reason, recent years have seen the combination of tropical species—in particular, orchids—with temperate blooms in the same display.

THIS PAGE
Clusters of white amaryllis mimic the shape of the chandelier.

OPPOSITE
A bounty of oriental lilies, white eustoma, white Tineke roses, white stocks and Vendela roses with viburnums. The trailing green ivy adds fluidity to the round arrangement. Adorning the base are posies of similar flowers, candles and loose petals.

This fusion of temperate and tropical is a source of surprise and delight for residents and guests at the Hotel, many of whom hail from temperate countries. Interesting touches like these make the various flower arrangements a conversation piece for many who see them, and Raffles Hotel a place for floral inspiration.

But even as he experiments in his arrangements, the Resident Florist is always mindful of certain guiding principles. While there are no fixed rules for flower arranging, each display should achieve a certain aesthetic aim. It should relate to the look, size and shape of its setting, and be in keeping with the style and mood of the occasion. Even the simplest-looking arrangement is the result of thoughtful design.

Little wonder then that the flowers leave an indelible impression on residents and visitors alike, and form part of the pleasurable memories that come from residing, dining and celebrating at Raffles Hotel.

settings

Settings are an important factor in determining the character of any floral arrangement. At the Raffles, floral gems are set in the grandeur of the lobby, the intimacy of the suites, and a diversity of dining venues.

The lobby is the first stop for visitors, and a popular backdrop to many a tourist snap. In this space exuding history and luxury, a large floral display takes centrestage. As befits a space with a crystal chandelier and a handwoven Persian rug, both the vase and arrangement are traditional, perhaps with some long stalks acting as counterpoints to the graceful columns. To match the dark wood and oriental carpet, flowers in rich, intense hues are favoured.

For those staying at the Hotel, smaller displays beckon in private lobbies and alcoves. For example, an arrangement in the lift lobby might comprise many different types of flowers. Recognising that this strategic location subjects the display to intense scrutiny, the Resident Florist provokes curiosity and conversation by using more eye-catching blooms such as extremely long-stemmed roses, or exotic flowers like anthuriums, vanda orchids and protea.

THIS PAGE
A display of pink oriental lilies, ornamental onions, cymbidium orchids and steel grass in the lobby. Delphiniums add height.

OPPOSITE
Anthuriums, alliums, white oriental lilies, round-headed leeks, foxtail lilies and hydrangeas at the private lobby. Leaves from irises, butcher's brooms and Swiss cheese plants provide foliage.

PAGE 16
The fluidity and vibrancy of yellow calla lilies.

PAGE 18
Pink hyacinths in a glass bowl, with accents of moss and lotus pods.

THIS PAGE
An ant plant vine is the base on which white and pink peonies with white hypericums, viburnums, Dark Blue Magic vandas and a collar of cast-iron plant leaves are painstakingly inserted.

OPPOSITE
Green hydrangeas are teamed with lotus pods and loops of steel grass in a green arrangement. For a dash of colour, moth orchids are pinned between the hydrangeas.

Suites at Raffles Hotel are famously refined and understated, with their dark wood flooring and antique furnishings. Flowers simultaneously brighten and soften the look of these living quarters; a gorgeous brush of colour and hint of fragrance add to the romance of a stay here. Most suites are adorned with live, potted moth orchids, a delicate-looking but resilient orchid indigenous to Southeast Asia.

A profusion of flowers is found in all seven Grand Hotel Suites. While the quintessential English rose still has its place, some of the arrangements are eclectic and contemporary. For example, green arrangements, which have been in vogue in recent years, may be featured. Live plants are also sometimes mixed with cut flowers, allowing part of the display to be re-used after the cut flowers are discarded.

THIS PAGE (LEFT)
Siam tulips, calla lilies and moth orchids—which last well out of water—are tied to pink hydrangeas.

THIS PAGE (BELOW)
An arrangement of white calla lilies, viburnums and cast-iron plants.

OPPOSITE
Dark Blue Magic vanda on a bed of viburnums and a crystal anthurium leaf. The leaf shape is repeated by bending bear grass into a heart. As a final detail, white hypericum berries are pierced onto the grass.

Orchids are the most commonly requested flower for the in-suite displays, perhaps because they are both exotic and synonymous with tropical Singapore. These flowers feature in many displays, and can be found perched on tables and washstands. Occasionally, the arrangements are spiced up by using a rare species of orchid, such as the Dark Blue Magic vanda. With its deep colour and dramatic markings, it needs only the simplest accompaniment to achieve maximum effect. For example, a single bloom might be posed on a single heart-shaped anthurium leaf to form a stunning escort for an in-room meal.

Besides orchids, lilies are popular requests. Some residents, however, have more particular instructions, such as 'white flowers only' or 'cut dendrobium orchids', all of which are faithfully met by the Resident Florist. The Raffles' Butler team also pays close attention to such preferences, noting them for future visits. This way, a repeat visitor to the Hotel will always be greeted with his or her favourite flowers.

THIS PAGE
Majestic Red calla lilies with gloriosa lilies match the colour of the china at Raffles Grill. Steel grass pierced with hypericum berries accents this simple arrangement that does not clutter the small table.

OPPOSITE
Traditional vertical arrangements of Peruvian lilies and butcher's broom foliage occupy silver bud vases at Raffles Grill.

Dining at Raffles is always meant to be a pleasing and memorable experience, whether residents and visitors opt for casual afternoon tea at Tiffin Room or a more formal evening dinner at Raffles Grill. While food remains the focus, careful attention is also paid to the entire ambience within each restaurant. And flowers are, without a doubt, an essential part of the equation.

A number of factors influence the floral displays on a dining table. Such considerations may include the size of the table, the overall colour scheme of the room, the china and even the upholstery.

At Raffles Grill, with its elegant, fine-dining setting, every table enjoys its own flowers. On an intimate table for two or four, space is a constraint. Therefore, a more vertical floral display is appropriate.

THIS PAGE
A single yellow calla lily held in place by a collar of palm leaf is multiplied for greater effect.

OPPOSITE
A posy of banksia, mini cymbidium orchids, moth orchids, gloriosa lilies and air plants is guaranteed to be a conversation piece.

The most straightforward of these displays is a solitary stem in a sleek vase. For such arrangements, flowers that work well on their own are chosen. Examples are Peruvian lilies and calla lilies. Because fine wine is often part of the dining experience at Raffles Grill, strongly scented blooms such as lilies and roses are avoided as their fragrance can interfere with the bouquet of the wine.

On a larger table, several vases with single blooms may be grouped to create the illusion of volume without clutter, or a more elaborate display with a greater variety of species may be used. Here again, the Resident Florist deftly mixes exotic blooms like Australian banksias (a spiny wildflower), tropical orchids and temperate flowers. Such combinations serve as conversation-starters for a convivial dinner.

occasions

Witnesses at births, weddings and other celebrations, flowers seem to be present at every major milestone in life. Unique floral creations contribute to the romance and glamour of an event, making each special occasion even more memorable.

THIS PAGE (RIGHT)
Gloriosa lilies, white roses and ivy adorn a cake.

THIS PAGE (BELOW)
Roses, milkweed, gloriosa lilies and hare's ear.

OPPOSITE
Hanging amaranthus, white oriental lilies, freesias and viburnums.

PAGE 30
White moth orchids on a bed of white hypericum berries and air plants.

PAGE 32
White roses on baby's breath, tied with lily grass.

Weddings, flowers and romance are a heady combination. And at Raffles Hotel, no effort is spared to conjure up the dream wedding.

This joyous occasion might take the form of a festive garden party with a fountain playing behind floral arches, a moving twilight ceremony in a flower-bedecked gazebo, or a lavish sit-down banquet in a flower-filled Jubilee Lounge. Some couples opt for tropical flowers, while others prefer imported blooms, although it is typical Raffles style to marry both. Roses are a perennial favourite, with easily 1,000 stalks used up in a weekend of weddings. Lilies and hydrangeas are also popular for their soft, romantic colours.

Making the flowers look unique for every wedding is important. One method is to differentiate where and how the flowers are used. Among the permutations and combinations are floral decorations on the wedding cake, displays along the processional aisle, candles encircled with fresh flowers, and an infinite variety of table displays.

The bridal bouquet is always highly personalised, with the Resident Florist taking pains to ensure it complements the bridal gown. For hand-tied bouquets it is very important that the flowers are carefully selected and properly conditioned in order to prolong the lifespan of such bouquets. For example, orchids hold up well without moisture while more fragile blooms need a water source. Seasonal blooms, such as peonies, are a good alternative.

THIS PAGE (ABOVE LEFT)
A bouquet of Dark Blue Magic vandas with white mini calla lilies.

THIS PAGE (ABOVE RIGHT)
Sounding a celebratory note, a wine bucket holds this posy of white roses, viburnums and ami maju.

OPPOSITE
A fragrant posy of white Tineke roses, viburnums and lisianthuses.

THIS PAGE
These burgundy calla lilies are bound with cast-iron plant leaves that also last for hours under the sun.

OPPOSITE
In this unconventional arrangement, cast-iron plant leaves are folded and immersed in water. The protruding leaf stalks become an interesting backdrop for the rare slipper orchid.

Events are opportunities for Raffles Hotel's team of florists to exercise artistic freedom. Working with the client or event organiser, the team conceptualises displays to match the theme of the event. At the annual Wine, Food & Arts Experience, in particular, the florists indulge in more expressive creations. In the spirit of the event, flowers may be arranged in avant garde, quirky designs.

Regardless of how unusual the arrangements are, the usual guideline of choosing flowers to fit the setting applies. Outdoor functions require hardier blooms that can withstand heat and moisture loss for the duration of the event. And when floral displays appear alongside objets d'art, the former are not allowed to steal the limelight, but rather, their mission is to enhance the art pieces on show.

THIS PAGE (RIGHT)
Mini-wreaths of myrtle with assorted berries.

THIS PAGE (BELOW)
A Christmas ornament twined with ant plant vine.

PAGE 40
This massive display consists of many small arrangements. Red roses mix with viburnum berries, mini apples, eucalyptuses, Christmas foliage and gold-sprayed camellia leaves.

Christmas sees Raffles Hotel decked in seasonal finery. An impressive Christmas tree—delivered in the small hours—is fully trimmed by 7am. Residents wake up, wander out of their rooms and marvel at its sudden appearance.

The Hotel's Christmas decorations seldom depart from the traditional. As the year's end is also the season to eat, drink and be merry, the florists work especially closely with each of the restaurants. Each year, a different colour theme is set, and the colour of the tablecloths is the starting point. Floral displays are designed to match. To inspire Yuletide cheer, the displays may feature Christmas ornaments.

The flowers are perhaps at their grandest at the Raffles' Annual Gala Christmas Tree Auction. This yearly charity event is attended by the President of Singapore and other society luminaries. No expense is spared for the festive flower arrangements, which include wintry elements: pine cones and needles, myrtle and mistletoe, all imported for the occasion.

gardens

The historic gardens of Raffles Hotel exude a quiet dignity. Amid the lush expanse of greenery, lovely tropical flowers provide the occasional splash of colour and a whiff of exotic fragrance.

THIS PAGE
Serene and secluded, the historic Palm Court is restricted to Hotel residents and staff.

OPPOSITE
The frangipani of Palm Court sheltered Somerset Maugham while he wrote.

PAGE 42
Colourful and striking heliconia are among the tropical flowers dotting the Hotel grounds.

PAGE 44
The fiery peacock flower blooms continually.

The gardens, which occupy a quarter of Raffles Hotel's land area, were returned to their original glory during the 1989 restoration of the hotel. They vary in character: Fern Court looks almost jungle-like; The Lawn, with its timber gazebo, is ideal for outdoor weddings; Palm Garden boasts an ornamental cast-iron fountain from the 1890s; while Palm Court (the Hotel's oldest garden) is stately and manicured.

Guests experience the gardens in various ways: touring them, dining in them, or viewing them from the shady verandahs. One denizen who made good use of the gardens was the British author Somerset Maugham. Legend has it that during his stays at the Raffles in 1926 and 1959, he would sit beneath a frangipani tree in the morning, spinning stories out of snatches of overheard gossip.

Sir Stamford Raffles, whom Raffles Hotel is named after, was a keen botanist and would have been familiar with the plants in the gardens. Of the 110 species, the three most associated with the Hotel are the traveller's palm, the footstool palm and the frangipani. These line the façade and encircle the Palm Court. The traveller's palm acquired its name because water trapped between its fronds could be drunk by thirsty travellers.

Reaching a height of up to 14 metres, the footstool palms appear like towering sentinels over the Hotel. Some of these hardy specimens have survived since the 19th century, and great pains were taken to preserve them during the restoration of the gardens. In contrast to these are the delicate-looking frangipani trees, which were planted—and continue to be much appreciated—for their aromatic flowers that bloom throughout the year.

THIS PAGE
Footstool palms tower over the bust of Singapore's founder, Sir Thomas Stamford Raffles.

OPPOSITE
Traveller's palms and footstool palms in the aptly named Palm Garden.

The extensive grounds are under the care of the Resident Horticulturist and five gardeners. They tend to more than 55,000 tropical plants, including ferns such as bird's nest and staghorn, spices such as ginger, and fruit trees such as banana, breadfruit and mango. While most are endemic to Southeast Asia, some were transplanted from far-flung lands in colonial times.

Over the years, a few new species have been introduced in the gardens, including flowering plants in selected locations such as The Lawn. Providing a splash of colour in the mostly green gardens are some stunning blooms, such as canna, wild ginger, lantana, peacock flower and heliconia. So, whether strolling through the buildings or the Hotel grounds, residents and guests are likely to encounter the Hotel's flowers.

THIS PAGE
Flowers found in the gardens include: (from left) red ginger, lantana and lobster claw.

OPPOSITE
The lush heart of the hotel, The Lawn is the perfect venue for many a private event.

Linus Loh, a member of the American Institute of Floral Designers, is the creative force behind every floral display at Raffles. Half of his floristry career has been spent with the Hotel, where he oversees 'routine' flower arrangements and floral extravaganzas for special events. Aside from his daily responsibilities, Linus is constantly on the lookout for new ideas, scouring flower markets whenever he travels.

Louie Fong graduated from the Singapore Botanic Gardens' School of Horticulture. Prior to becoming the Hotel's Resident Horticulturist in 2000, he planned, designed and managed floral and plant displays for Changi International Airport. There, his creations welcomed thousands of travellers to Singapore, the Garden City. Today, Louie expertly and lovingly tends the idyllic gardens of Raffles Hotel.

Explore the world of flowers and learn to recognise what you like. When you travel, visit the local flower stalls and gardens for new ideas.

Purchase your flowers when fresh shipments have just arrived. In Singapore, the best days are Mondays, Wednesdays and Saturdays. Sunday is the worst day to buy flowers anywhere in the world.

Select flowers that are in season and when they do not cost a fortune. Feel free to ask the florist for advice. Most love their work and enjoy discussing their products.

Know what you are buying. Tulips don't last more than five days even in the cool European climate. In the tropics, native flowers last longest, with fresh-cut orchids lasting for up to two weeks.

Choose just one type of flower for a quick and foolproof arrangement at home. Confining yourself to one flower type creates a neat and simple focus. If you prefer a more colourful arrangement, buy the same variety of flower in various hues or shades.

Pick colours appropriate to the setting and that will help achieve the mood you are aiming for. For example, in a room full of neutral tones, brightly coloured blooms make for a cheerful highlight, while pale-coloured flowers serve as a subtle accent.

Cut flowers with a sharp knife or scissors, as only a sharp, even cut will let the stems absorb water efficiently. This keeps your blooms fresher for longer.

Revive newly bought flowers by cutting their stems under water. This works especially well for sunflowers and chrysanthemums, which usually come wrapped up and curled.

Save surplus blooms and recycle old ones. A solitary leftover flower makes an elegant statement on a dresser, vanity top or dining table. Even broken flower heads can be put to good use—simply float them in a bowl, with or without candles, or scatter them in the tub for a sensual bath.

Experiment with foliage. Twigs and leaves can enhance a display without distracting from the flowers. If you are feeling adventurous, try composing an arrangement completely out of foliage.

Use whatever you have on hand at home as receptacles. Cups and saucers, bottles and bowls can double up as attractive vessels for flowers. You don't need an antique Ming vase—let the beautiful blooms be the focal point.

Aim for balance and proportion. An oversized floral display can end up overwhelming a small space, while too modest an arrangement can fade into oblivion in a large room.

Place your floral arrangements in a cool spot, away from direct sunlight, hot lights and appliances. This will help them to stay beautiful for longer.

Change the water in vases every day or add cut flower preservatives, especially if the weather is hot and humid. This prevents bacterial growth in the water, which can be detrimental to flower stems. Cloudy water indicates bacteria and must be discarded.

Create bouquets for any occasion, not just weddings. A homemade bouquet is a thoughtful and personalised gift for your host.

Take care when using flowers with or on food. Use them sparingly and wash them first, as most flowers have been sprayed with pesticides. Definitely avoid sappy flowers, stems or leaves. Edible, organically grown flowers are safest.

Incorporate a water source in bouquets—hand-tied bouquets are charming but dehydrate more quickly, especially in hot weather.

Grow your own plants and flowers if you can. Even without a garden, a few potted plants will do wonders for the atmosphere in your home. If you suffer from hay-fever, opt for non-flowering plants.

Consider other plant parts too, like pods, fruit and twigs. Some fruit convey a seasonal mood, such as pumpkins in the fall, and apples at Christmas. They can be fresh, dried or even artificial.

Enjoy your flowers while they last. Having put your heart into growing a plant, arranging a display or assembling a bouquet, you deserve that satisfaction.